OUT THERE

Also by Elsa Corbluth

St Patrick's Night (Peterloo Poets, 1988)
The Planet Iceland (Peterloo Poets, 2002)
The Hill Speaks (Jurassic Press, 2008)

Elsa Corbluth has won a number of poetry prizes,
including in the Arvon, the National, the Bridport, Cheltenham,
Yorkshire, Apricot Gold and Poetry on the Lake (Italy).

Her work has also been read on BBC Radio 3 and 4

Acknowledgements

Acknowledgements are due to the editors of the following
publications in which some of these poems first appeared:
*Outposts, Xenia, Language Matters,
Samphire, Meridian, Word and Action*

For my friends the Harbour Poets

- past present and future

Out There – Elsa Corbluth

First Edition 2010

ISBN 9780955060564

© Elsa Corbluth 2010

Cover design and Layout © Bardic Media 2010

Set in Georgia

Published by Bardic Media Ltd
2 Hardy Cottages, School Lane
West Lulworth, Wareham, Dorset BH20 5SA

Printed and bound by Copytech (UK) Ltd
Peterborough

www.bardicmedia.co.uk

Out There

Elsa Corbluth

On Elsa Corbluth's previous books:

St Patrick's Night
The title poem won joint first prize in the Cheltenham poetry competition and several other poems in this collection won prizes.

The Planet Iceland
'Here the imagery is so strong you could think your eyes filled with icicles...it's all about mystery and the mastery of words and Elsa Corbluth certainly has both these gifts.'

Tim Harris, *South*

'The book is haunted by a pagan numinousness, as though something of the old soul of Iceland has got into the poet's persona.'

Herbert Lomas, *Ambit*

The Hill Speaks
'*The Hill Speaks* is powerful, often painful stuff...a very reliable writer, Corbluth has a distinguished record of prizewinning. This collection, like her earlier work, is vividly alive.'

Dr R V Bailey, *Envoi*

'I like her poetry. There is a directness and a toughness about it which grabs one immediately. And wit. And the mix of demotic and lyrical.'

Piers Plowright

"OUT THERE is a selection of poems not seen in my other collections, with a central theme not related to me. They were written over many years – the ones that were topical are now historical, but history doesn't date. Some events or characters are less well known, but are still, in some sense, OUT THERE."

Elsa Corbluth

April 2010

Out There – Elsa Corbluth

Contents

Swan Dance	- 11
Refugee Child	- 13
Guy Fawkes Night	- 14
The House by the Canal	- 15
Aberfan, from Abbotsbury	- 17
Splashdown	- 20
A Girl Shot	- 25
Vietnamese Gods	- 27
Group Criticism	- 29
The Man	- 31
No	- 32
Emergency Poem	- 33
What Colour is Summer?	- 35
Icetime	- 37
Funeral Without Bereaved	- 38
Word Game	- 40
Accident	- 46
Poem to a Collage of Food and Fatness	- 47
Overheard on a Writing Course	- 49
Out There	- 50
The Christian Witch	- 51
People who Carve	- 53
A Choice	- 54

Contents (cont...)

What does the Paint Blot Say?   - 55

Genaka   - 57

Darl Bundren Talks with Himself   - 61

Defence   - 66

The Heavensent Tearooms   - 67

Ultimatum   - 70

The Rail God   - 71

Kangchenjunga   - 73

Some News Items:

The Bouncy Church   - 76

The Bread Summit   - 77

Winter Walking, USA   - 79

Stogumber   - 80

Swan Dance
(Alicia Markova dances Pavlova's 'Dying Swan')

Her whiteness is not the whiteness of snow or of swift water,
Of summer cloud or any pale spring flower,
Of moonlit swan or sun-encircled seagull
But white fire,
Slow rippling, quivering, swift uprush of fire:
She, a flame,
White flame needs neither tongue nor eyes to tell
Her birth and death and immortality.
There is laughter in her heels, but not for us;
Her fingers do not smile in this blue night
Her white toes pierce. Her sobbing feet
Move the blue darkness: see how her hands weep!
We are her eyes and she their white-hot tears
Given for us, falling into the night.
We are her voice and she the tongue that cries
Exultant pain, white steel-thrust in the darkness.

She is at times the moon, and we, losing identity,
Become as walls, as trees against the sky.
She moves, the moon, across the cardboard walls of houses
In the blue night,
Lighting with soft ridicule the flat and brittle trees.

Now from her floating disc the slender flame
Springs:
Poised like a pause in breath our fingers, tense,
Now flicker in her anguish and are still.

We know her stories
Of swans, of love-lorn girls and green wood spirits,
But if we see her burning she will tell us
Tales out of time.

She droops: the bird-wing, petal, yacht-sail bends,
Snaps lightly, crumbles, falling into time.
She lives, and in the sudden daylight framed
She is a mountain top, a wave, a dancer.

Out in the naked night
The road shines and the silver walkers move
With unaccustomed grace,
Smooth-limbed as winter plane trees and their hands
As plane leaves rise and fall.
They are the city's seasons and its end
And in their round dark eyes the white fires burn.

1950

Refugee Child
(Photograph in 'Picture Post')

All day the frost stayed where the shadows were
And faces hurt with little pins of cold
And breath blew whiter than the night's-old snow.

Who is the woman not my mother
Crying a smile with some teeth gone
Like some of the windows in the town?

Snow bunched wet on the grass,
Raw trees, the sky soft mud,
The road tops matted with sky.
The road is ten years long.

1956

Guy Fawkes' Night

Children, shoot your stars, the world is burning.
Blood-light towns!
Children, fire your dreams, the night is raining
Splintered suns!

Who is your favourite guy?
Everyone has somebody to burn.

So light him up until your eyes are blazing
And your feet war-dancing
And your hands clap-clapping,
Sticks snapping, and your hair blown flares!

Children, live your flames, and glow together
Before they burn you, one way or another.

1956

The House by the Canal
(between Nottingham and Derby)

Who lives there who is warm enough inside him
Warm in his work, his wife and with the constant rub of children
To defy year-long Novembers
Clung round his walls and to the heavy fields
And steaming from the flat brown water?

Who, when fog rattles from the morning trees,
Has heart enough to face the drag of dawn
Drowned into evening without noticeable day?

Who, when one morning out of ten
The penny sun is spun
Over the flat flood stretches to reveal his native land,
Would not hanker for his native fog's return
That gave at least a pearl-like mystery
To the lost land behind the ticking trees?

For when light coils like rusted wire
Around strange clouds
The tired hills put forth
Thin waifs of villages to grow
Black-toothed, wet-hard as coal;
Far chimneys thumb the overbearing sky,
Thin into ghosts before new-coming rain.

Who is so warm that he has learned to keep
Heart above water?

Or is it cold that he must be to weather
Blurred muffled days and brown unwarming suns,
His work unloved
And moving like the sluggish breath of fog,
His wife numb as the ghost of living water,
His children stilled flood-ponds?

Or is he old as coal, is he alone
As a house in a fog,
To bear the ageing air,
Daily to turn his flat flood-puddle eyes
To smudge of trees behind his grey-white gate,
The white-grey sky sunk down, right down to their roots,
And planting pin-head drops upon
His whitening grey hair?

1958

Aberfan, from Abbotsbury

And is it raining in the other valley?
(Here, stone and rain are gold and the cold mellow).
Is the rain black on the falling mountain?

Pit wives who keep some small space held for death
At the back of their lives,
Some little hollows ready in their faces
For patience in a necessary pause
That any day they may be asked to breathe through,
Know, as they make their fire in the smudged morning,
That their smudged hands might be, by the same evening,
Mothers' and fathers' to their clamouring children.

Even there is some waiting in their shoulders
As a son, school done, takes his snap-box
Into his first pit's anaesthetic morning.

The valley will have given him
Fifteen years of smirched sun and blacked snow,
A lore and a belonging and some laughing,
Whatever, for her future, stands above him
In his slag of sky.

But not for him at five,
Not as she ties his shoelace,
Buttons his neck against the mist
And hustles him to school.
"He's in good hands."
And school sings out its day's beginning:
For thine is the kingdom.

And her girls,
Knitted into bright sleeves for the winter,
Hair grown through the long yard-skipping,
Ditch-fishing, rubble-clambering holiday
To keep their necks from the slap of the dark wind?
She will expect to mother them through labours,
To rock and dummy their fat babies at her back door.
She will expect her girls.

She will expect her children home from school.

(One night last winter
My four-year daughter sat up crying, crying
"I don't like dying."
A playground witch of six to Sleeping Beauty
Had said "You'll die at five."
I told her "Not until you're very old."
She slept, consoled).

And the Pied Piper called all the children into the hill
For ever and ever.

(Even here falls the cold.
Our children, tanned like this stone,
From a whole summer's shingle sliding,
Foam tumbling, driftwood building, run
Out of the storm
Under the hanging downs to their warm school,
Safe from sea's rearing in their lit classroom.)

While down that valley cuts the sharp slate rain.

1966

Splashdown (Apollo 13)

Washed white by fear,
millions, suspended,
stared
at the square window,
eyes to its eye
engaged,
ears to its tuning
into the hollowed,
the metalled down voices
of the three white ones,
the precious,
the smooth-headed,
cool-fingered
rare ones,

to gaze again,
as though stung eyes
could will the three to sight,
ears strain them into range.

Carpet with blood
the piece of deck they walk
from bloodless danger,

three small grey men
who have not grown grotesque
or glorified with some unearthly gleam.

Three neutral coloured
upright ones, our kind,
hinting unsteadiness
in our own element,
meet the trite amplified
prayer from the dazzling crisp
white figures sent to meet them.

Who sat up there,
what bland immaculate
shaven jehovah
with faintly knotted temples,
posted at what infallible controls,
eternally receiving
such brisk communications?

Do not switch off.
Those rows of sky-white and four-cornered eyes
may yet cry blood.
We have not yet seen all.

Show us again
three mushroom tops

sway gently down,
horizon dip and thrust,
and real men swim
with primates' hands,
no switch to operate
the final linking.

This is a birth without a child,
a drowning with no corpse.

Do not hear bitterness
in this, envy of otherness.
To have routed the high snow,
read fantasies as children,
is to accept the journeys
"Beyond the last blue mountain..."

Earth navigators
and earth mountaineers
can afford fear:
all shades and changes of the coloured world
will allow grief,
but on the grey moon's
dry seas,
airless mountains,
there is the grey stage set
for cliché ultimate.

A cosmic misadventure
brings all men shoulders close:
it seems that, otherwise,
men have not shoulders.

Men must be driven out
beyond air and their weight
for men to feel man's weight
and breathe for men.

Stroke them with sunlight,
lap them with long sleep,
toss them the taste of sea.

It is our turn for pain,
so tilt relief
that every pausing
in the green of day
is clear with tears.

And will their women hold
their sleek heads like stabbed birds'
that have death on their eyes,
or will they too be given,
and give, these new-moon smiles?

Most women ride
the farther spaces
to complete a child,
splash down from where
no man has gone
since his first landing.

Though every shooting grain
that cracks earth's skin
breaks nearer to man's stars,
yet men must still
print the dead moon
or desperately
burn,
rather than dare
the human temperature.

1970

A Girl Shot
(Kent, Ohio, May 1970)

It was a face
treasured by fingertips
and risen in the spring,
opened magnolia.

They have drilled a hole in the sun
and sent crying
to the metalled roof of night
her live father,
set in his every part
electrodes of grief.
The current enters us.

They have burned her,
the white witch;
she is smoking
to anyone's heaven.
They have put out
her wide dark seeing,
spined with steel thorns
her dark dropped hair,

smartly, as in sport:
it could have been a deer,
silk bird ripped from silk air:
today it was a girl.
Let blood close over us.

1970

Vietnamese Gods

They made bridges
like harp strings
for their thin
attenuated gods,
the fragile wisps
that tiptoed across
charmed rice,
spinning invisible
films of protection
over the pale-feather crop
and its lean brown
guardians,
the steady bowing
of round roof-hats,
the rhythmic worship
of their work, the whispered
incantation of water
and trickling grains of music.

There came thick
booted gods
with different rituals.
They made a pyre
of dry house roofs,
the flames quick to take root,

and of all those
hair-thin spirits,
fizzing them out, to leave
a thin brown lost
people, aghast,
who did not also go
out like smoke
after the new
and heavy god legs
had strode through
their web-fine bridges.

1970

Group Criticism

A corrugated paper poet
uncrumpled a poem.
Creased as it was
he rustled it to us.

We were supposed to have come
to the book-packed room
to tear it to bits for him,
then heap it up,
tip it back
into the top of his head,

or beat it to papier-maché
and stick it all over him
to firm him up again;

so he didn't look thumbed
or dog-eared
as might have been feared,
but with some of his dents
even blown out, he sat
almost as if the loose,
loose leaves of his life
were already a book.
Yes, we were hard

covers for him,
even those of us whose
ball points of eyes
had made little holes in him.

Meanwhile the wind
shook the reflected
wallfuls of books
in the window behind him.

1971

The Man

There was a man and he could dissolve clouds.
He could turn them to soapsuds, into unwanted hair.
He would stare and stare until they were no longer there
but all the blue air.

There was a man and he could remove mountains,
gesture rocks into slices of cake and bring rain to eat them.
With a flick of his wrist he would shake caves inside out,
hang their tonsils out.

There was a man and this man could stride back tides,
shrug rivers uphill, blink lakes to a network of mudcracks,
spike the sun on his fork and have it for his breakfast,
pack stars in sackfuls.

There was a man and he could dissolve people.
He looked them into the distance and wasted their words.
He thought he loved them. They had been thinking he loved them.
He thought they loved him.

1972

No

Her strong brown house, planted like a fist in the lane,
was now sucked backwards into littleness
like a child's spat-out boiled sweet, very pale.

The hill that crouched over the house
was clear with coming rain,
furrows and starred wires that were part of him.

The sea beyond her house
turned over and scolloped down on him
with terrible gold.

He tried lying on the brown afternoon sand
with all his clothes on
in front of the hut that said "Lost Children",
pretending summer,

but the lead night sea
slopped in sour with seaweed

and lights were leaking over the promenade
like gas escapes someone had lit with a match.

1973

Emergency Poem

In the new year there will have to be poetry cuts.

All poems unfinished on December the thirty-first
will go into cold storage.

But if somebody switches off to economise
you had better beware:
how would you like to have poems running about the streets?

In public halls
there will be children knocking over poems:
it won't be easy to mop poems up.

Old people when they spread
their butter concessions
may discover a little bit of poetry
left on the knife.

The flustered housewife opening a tin
may find, silly of her,
that she has served up to her family
poems on toast.

Poems will leave footprints all over the house
but you won't be able to find them.

Poems may be buried in gardens
but will shoot up out of hiding
and you won't be able to hold them.

Poems will even be born in telephone kiosks
and be put through to
automatic answering machines.

*(During the economy drive at this time a "corpse" being
transported in a vehicle which had its refrigeration switched off to
economise, woke up.)*

1973

What Colour is Summer?
(in a coastal village)

Is it red?
Eyelid's glow in the shingle bed.

Is it blue?
Skylight of love that pulses through.

Is it gold?
Noon sun for the sea to hold.

Is it green?
Pasture where deep rain has been.

Is it mauve?
Wild orchids in an island cove.

Is it grey?
Day like a cave and a tail of spray.

Is it white?
Lily wreath for a wedding night.

Is it black?
Moon-faced bride with the night on her back.

Is it cream?

Dead woman's face in the gulp of a dream.

Is it clear?

Backwater's length in an old man's tear.

Is it all?

Rainbow to hold back the pall.

1974

Icetime (A 70's view of climate change)

When frisky rivers cut to icicles
and hungers come down from their posters
into fitted kitchens
will you and you and I be left holding
ideas on a stick like ice-lollies?

Let us eat ice. Let us eat our words.
When we scrabble for seeds
in the paper soil
shall we pull out songs,
sing ourselves to sleep?

Tonight we will sleep
in a snowing forest,
lie down with the dogs
of our thoughts,
sink under our
blanket of cold.

And what-voiced beast shall come
in the next thaw
to dig out man prints
in a six-foot wide
rock sandwich?

1974

Funeral Without Bereaved

They couldn't shut the doors fast enough.
We stood in winter coats chastened
by our January daffodils
put out of sight efficiently by pulleys.

At the raw edge of the out of season
seaside town our village vicar
who like us had got up early
and driven slowly through the steel-wool morning

to say the words said we should "not *prev*ent him"
and none of us wanted to.
I am wondering which kind of mourning
will haunt us for longest,

the shivering girl widow,
dumb mother moaning for her smashed son,
red blubbering man whose wife turned in mid-life
into an orange rose in this flower bed

or these kindly practical
joky neighbours doing the decent thing
for the street's old nuisance,
no family that counted or laid claim to

any leftover sadness. The last words I heard him
spill from that mouth that neighbours
quietened with little puddings like a conscience
were "see the   bodies   burning."

1975

Word Game
(A short history of literacy, or before and after Scrabble)

"In the beginning was the Word".

Before the beginning
the small, shelled things were sucked to rocks,
fungus fastened to treetrunks,
air howled or was suspended,
snow snarled itself to pieces in the light
and the night
stuck it together again.

In the beginning were gods
and whatever were there
before the first people
blew gods into the air
like balloons of breath
on cold days,
the jolly-bellied, the fierce-nosed,
even the female, all circles,
arranged like apples.

In a beginning was God,
God the male,
God of superior muscles.
With a blow of his fist he sent all the other gods packing.

(They were not quite banished:
now and then they were going to surface
in old gossips, young girls, black cats, red spiders
or some far innocent star.)

He said (because He was God-the-Word)
Now I am the only
(Child? Father? Son?)
I have done away with
all superfluous relatives.
There is one Word.
It is   Me.

In the beginning was the child
whose mouth pumping her flesh
defined his world's end.
The weaned child
picked the brains of the wise men,
spat out the indigestibles.
After that plain men
let go their nets, turned loose their animals
and followed him to the ends of his words.

Next, instead of an eye for an eye,
it was ten thousand eyes
for each saint's glass one.
Instead of a word for a word

it was a testament,
for every word let fall
a manifesto.
Men snuffed each other out
not for food or for women
but for words.
And when they had the words?
Burnt them up, they were not the ones that they wanted.

The Lord Word
learned to speak in every language:
(*Sieg Heil!*)
and every dialect of every language.
A Californian accent was one of his favourites;
Etonian, Cape Town or Belfast, you name it.
His Russian was fluent
(the Word was not necessarily
always religious.)

Now and then the Word exploded in a pillarbox.

The Word grew schizophrenic
thinking itself not God
because so many people were starting to say so.

The God grew paranoid
feeling itself not Word
because more and more people were wanting
to do away with it.

Boys came out in words like pimples,
girls hung ropes of words around their necks.
It was, like, anarchy.

All the small gods started to come back.

In the end Word Almighty, psychopath,
threw his veto about and was taken away
with his definitions
and padlocked
in a family bible
the size of Australia.

When the word children
in their turn had children
these kept their tongues
as close as limpets.
Some taught their hands to read
the wires of small machines or rockface maps,
directions out of silence
on the strings of instruments.
The hands of others spoke to animals.

Some may have found their ways into each other:
It was after our time.

Every year there were fewer letters delivered.
Up and down the country it was difficult
to find a single bookshop.
Forests began to spread.
As books were lost from public libraries
they were replaced by rubber plants.
Television interludes
of water lily leaves and chamber music
became so long that plays and documentaries
averaged about five minutes
of speeded action.
There were angers of course,
the occasional handful of people
rushing about screaming and breaking windows.
There were even small-scale killings.
These were treated as natural disasters.
Funds were set up and compensation paid.
It was all done by mathematics.

We can't tell what happened after the end
as we weren't there and no records were kept
but we suspect it was something like
before the beginning,
tides inking the coastlines,

clays working away like printing presses
to type the bones of fishes,
whisper of eel grass, storm groans,
and the whole establishment
trembling at the edge of Word.

After the end
there could still have been time
for the process to begin.

1975

Accident

When the holds ran out
over blue space

from the face of the little grey guide book
open in the climber's head

and all that remained was the white
lightly pitted, green lichened
bulge of the overhang

the next colour was blood
(who would have expected
such a rush of it
out of a head's book?)

Then it was cold grey-white to mauve,
a bled face and a fell painted,
a fog singing, the head's way lost.

1975

Poem to a Collage of Food and Fatness

The anorexic's nightmare
is to be swollen as her pregnant mother
and to be large and old enough to bear
another greedy daughter.
She is not starved of care,
so, cosseted, she thrives upon her wasting
until, a sliver of her growing self,
she slithers back into the space that made her,

but the fat lady,
oh all alone,
the diners gone,
the snackers turned away,
has to keep chewing on her dreams of love.
Guzzling, she wallows in the fats and starches
that want her body
until no spaces haunt it
and she keels over, bloated,

while the true hungry,
the plate-eyed child
at the end of our donations,
can have no substance but its wholeness longing
to be minimally bigger than it is,

food love and love its food,
ballooning belly
blindly prepared for float-off.

1977

Overheard on a Writing Course

"Let's have the birds on the boughs and no more of all this filth."

"Even birds have bodies, don't forget,
bird brains, bird bowels:
eggs do not grow on trees,

and even trees have bodies,
trees
are most erotic:
their limbs dare
far more than ours,

their roots bared,
brazen forks,
bold folds and creases,

their gestures to the light,
their curves and curls
and stiffenings,

their messages that fire the throats of birds."

1978

Out There

There's enough hardware here,
pylons outgrowing trees,
ironmongery of oil
cluttering a coastscape,
litter, the obscene frills lining lanes,
and air exhausted
by summer drivers clogging their routes out,

and now there is the moon.
Manscape the moon,
lower wire spiders,
print with powered graffiti
your dustscape prize.

Somewhere inside your clever lifeline suit
there is a small,
a holed and pitted man
moon-riddled by the fears
more deep than space,
and there's a land unscaped
for him to pioneer.

1978

The Christian Witch

The Christian witch
whose steeple hat had stars,
who conjured queens
from cardboard boxes,
also conjured hope
from hopeless people
until her heart died.

Limbo, she dreamed,
was like a striped icecream,
but not in colour,
olive fawn and grey
of layered soil,
and in this no-heart's-land
her Christ upbraided her.

The magic pacemaker
bewitched her into light,
to face my pink bouquet,
when she had conjured Christ
out of his clay
and she had heard him say:

"To die of others' hurt
is not doing my work.

I did not ask to die:
I do not ask your death.
Accept my anger with my wizardry:
out of the grey of earth
I conjure back your breath."

1978

People Who Carve

People who carve on cliffs their predictable
messages and names assume that there will be
no landslip at that point.

People who carve the air from the cliffs' fringe
and ask for your remembrance by their end
assume they will be found.

People who find these shells of persons feel
the meat in them go cold.

There is no green but in the seeing lens,
sand but in touching hand.

1978

A Choice

You can journey to your guru
Who sits, a white jug pouring
His bland words into you
(Outside, the world is roaring.)

Honour his allergies,
Dress up like marmalade,
Dismiss the light of trees
At a hundred in the shade,

Reject the blue of seas
For the parched colours,
Leave the clouds' greys
And the greens that follow

For the brown sands
And paper reeds,
For the dry lands
And the dead seeds.

1979

What Does The Paint Blot Say? (Hubris)

Men Said
    Let there be gods
        and gods flew
      gold of the sky
    and green as poking grain
with such a scattering

      clay could have turned to stone
and sperm to bone.
      Then men were not alone.

Some gods were black,
  black runnıng blots
    like footsteps in the snow
      of nothing known
        or in the yellow sand
      of nothing planned.

    Their work was punishing
    men for their manness
    in not being gods
  yet men who took
the colours of the gods

and flew to meet them,
these had blackest ends.

But better Hades
    than the dark of dark
and better burning
    than the godless light?

1979

Genaka

I am Genaka. The name is Indian. It is mine. I was given it
by my Master at the Ashram, fat, bearded in white linen.
I was christened Gillian. I hardly ever think of it.
It was a long journey here. I came with my boyfriend.
A slow journey. Hot. Sick. Dust, smells, noises.
People. Panics and resignations. We travelled light.
As we went we grew lighter ourselves.
These orange trousers I bought before I came,
this orange shirt, orange socks and orange underwear.
By the time we arrived our skins were slightly orange.
This orange jumper I was given by a friend
on a brief visit home. It is synthetic.
The Master is allergic to wool. We must not wear it
in the cool evenings when we all gather
to hear his evening talks.
                          In England I felt strange,
quiet and alone. The Master had taken away
all my aggression and my interest in possessions.
I was kind and peaceful. I felt that I was liked,
but it was not the same. I had to go back,
this time alone. I had split from my boyfriend
but there was the Master and there were all the others,
all the same colour, understanding each other.
I worked hard, though less hard than some of them.
My work was clerical. We mailed his books

all over the world. Every morning talk
and every evening talk he gave was taped,
transcribed and printed. Every week or two a book.
I lost count. The husband of the woman
whose jumper I am wearing had several shelves full of them,
heavy glossy books with his photo on the cover.
(These were friends of my mother. We remet them after
twenty years, so I hadn't remembered them.
She knew them from the days when my father lived with us.)

It was good back here. I knew where I was, who I was.
I did not belong to myself. I was his.
I listened to him. Twice a day. The morning hour. The evening
hour.
All of us, orange. He, white and apart. He was There,
where we were all striving to be, some of us with difficulty,
cleansing ourselves of doubts, fears and divisions.
Every day I was dissolving into
that orange bloodstream, none of us dreaming of wearing
blue or green any more than questioning
his wisdom. We were sand to the white surf
of his words. It was almost perfect.
Occasionally he talked to me on my own,
and that was bliss. I was filled with a special strength
for days afterwards.

One day we met as usual
to listen to his talk for that day, and for the first time
we could not understand him. He said, in his usual voice,
"I am going away. I will build a bigger Ashram
somewhere else. You will find me there", and that was all.

We are spots of orange blood on a grey confusing river.
We are no longer together here or anywhere.
We are parched and colourless.
We are no-one. We have nowhere to go. We are shabby, hungry.
We are specks of orange dust on a huge wind,
some of us angry but impotent in our rages,
some of us weeping defenceless with no-one to comfort us.
Few of us have money. Food is running out. Many are ill.
None of us knows what to do. We have always had our instructions.
Some of us are begging or turning to prostitution.
There is no attempt to stay together, to continue.
We are nothing without him and he has left us.

Rumours trickle through. He has been seen in New York
in blue jeans. He is building a mansion
on the proceeds from his books. We are without centre,
without incentives. We are thousands,
the lowest caste in India. We have lost our language.
We are resented everywhere. We are useless.

I am Gillian Westwood. I am an English girl
in a foreign country. How can I get back?
I will write to my friends for money. I will write to the man
with those shelves of expensive books. I will write with affection
"My dearest Daniel". I met him only briefly.
Some of my friends know him, said that he went orange.
He's in the Cotswolds in a house of orange stone.
Their evening kitchen where I sliced the onions
fills with green light, scent of grass, cows, honeysuckle.
I will ask him for money, to be sent to the Ashram,
to Gillian Westwood. That is my legal name.
I will sign it, Genaka.

But the Ashram is closing.
Everyone is leaving. Thin waifs in faded orange
flicker through hostile streets. Will he answer my letter
before this is not an address? He is a busy man.
My leader has left. All the disciples are leaving.
The beautiful orange flower is a tattered rag, our soul's house
soulless, all the souls homeless. It is not likely Daniel,
will answer, or, if he does, that I will get the letter,
Ashram gone, Genaka gone, the orange sun
going down brown behind the dark back of India.

1981

Darl Bundren Talks With Himself

No darling
Darl
dead mother
under the tree
you smell her breathing
through the box's
holes

buzzards
black slow
sinking
moths,
or cobweb
cave bats
dripping
from the
sun

they know
that she
should
burn
no flood
has washed her
clean

and her
brood
rides her
whipped

the night
must spurt
her blaze of
blood

Darl
swirling
her scarlet
secret
on the
sky

but in the
cackling
barn
where I was
born

why
was she
not

left there to
lie?

my brother
is the
carpenter

my brother
straddles her
and her hoofs
beat

my brother is a child
he hooks her
slippery and cold

how many
brothers
hurt
inside my
head?

my sister's
baby
wails

through all
the walls

neighbours
avoid
us, pinching
thin their noses

and Darl
rises
no purple broken leg
no frizzled back
but inside his
head's box
is the hot black

she will be following
after spades have stopped
her with
her people's earth

from Darl's mouth foams
the curling river

now he has a mother
new as last year's

Thanksgiving
turkey

and that good father
who guided
all his people
to this pass

bares his brash teeth
old stallion
in the staring world's
mouth

wall Darl
in an
eiderdown
of silence

and sting him medicines
to take away
his dreams

(William Faulkner's novel,
As I Lay Dying)

1982

Defence

Meanwhile, missiles are still being piled.

"Little boy": the children ran to ribbons.
"Fat man": and the young girls' faces melted.
On steps to no door sits a stamped white outline,
seconds before, a person.

Now giant "men" are mustering underground,
ready to snow white light at the drop of a finger,
after the blinding red, before the arctic darkness.

Planet, defenceless
as an abused child, pinned to your habit of hope
like women who wait, moon after moon, by the starred wire,

will the brain-child you died to deliver
grow from you, a bleached tree? a dry river?
After the hot brain-blossom, will there be apples,
skins of all fruits, all creatures, all the peoples?

Would there be scent of wallflowers, grass spearing dew
or that cool hill, the sun's crimson camellia
fallen behind it, leaving the shuffling cattle?

Could there be waving legs and arms of babies
lying awake outdoors in summer looking at their hands?

1986

The Heavensent Tearooms
(for Caroline Olsen)

In the Heavensent Tearooms
the sponge is rather dry.
You wonder why?
It takes so long to come down from the sky.

In the Heavensent Tearooms
the scones are always stale
which tells a tale
of travelling distance on the light-years scale.

In the Heavensent Tearooms
you'll find the biscuits soft,
and if you've coughed
to complain, they'll say, "They come down from aloft."

In the Heavensent Tearooms
the tea is somewhat stewed
but it would be rude
to mention this. You know where it was brewed.

In the Heavensent Tearooms
The coffee is too weak,
but do not speak
of such a thing: it could cause a holy pique.

In the Heavensent Tearooms
the toast is often burned:
as you have learned
it passed through lightning and has not been turned.

In the Heavensent Tearooms
the waitresses, angelic,
daily dust each pastry relic
in case they may be called upon to sell it.

In the Heavensent Tearooms
you wait ages to be served.
If you're unnerved
by the management's remoteness - - space is curved.

In the Heavensent Tearooms
the clientèle's select,
which will affect
the atmosphere: it's not what you'd expect.

In the Heavensent Tearooms
the décor is divine:
a kind of shrine
with church-like mustiness and dust so fine.

In the Heavensent Tearooms
you are meant to fast.
Don't look aghast:
You're not the first customer and you won't be the last.

In the Heavensent Tearooms
they'll get to you in the end,
you and your friend,
even if it isn't in the way that you intend.

Oh the Heavensent Tearooms
are quite celestial,
ecclesiastical,
not a common caff, all jolly, comfy, bestial.

So let us all our voices raise
to these sacred Tearooms in a hymn of praise
and hold a mass for pious ones
with cool stale tea and tough old buns,
so that the Boss, with best intent,
will bless the Tearooms Heavensent.

(There was once a café called 'The Heavenscent Tearooms')

1989

Ultimatum
January 1991 (Film, *Apocalypse Now*)

Vietnam on the box. Outside, a gale raving.
Dance of the choppers, talk of the hacked children.
Here, half a moon fells a tree, garden yelling.
There, it's not merely a film. It was. It may soon be.
Here roars a real wind. There rage filmed fire storms
searing late night eyes, here. These windows rumble.

Next day the wind's dropped. Moon's half-circle
axe stands in dayrise pink. Bland screened faces,
proxy arsonists with touch-paper hands,
repeat, no quarter, no third way. Each new day
counts down to attack by the cowboy technicians.

Modern warfare's like AIDS, you can't have a touch of it.
Peace talk is a winter rose. You cannot have too much of it.

1991

The Rail God

decrees:
to have fail-safe signalling
would not be
cost-effective.

Therefore, a mere twenty-seven,
every so often,
with terminal
lacerations

is a calculated
factor in the balancing
of the economy:

your auntie,
off to the city
on a pensioners'
special offer,

your pre-school grandson
taking Teddy
to the seaside
on a family ticket,
student daughter or son

pocketing railcard,
dumping rucksack...

In Zurich
where trains run on time
and time is traded and valued
it would not be thought tidy,

even once in a year,
to litter the tracks
with jagged broken

life-sized toys,
splashes of customers'
blood, disturb the crisp
air with moaning.

It is said the Swiss
have no sense of humour.

Oh but we have:
switch on any time:

see the railway jokes
brought out
on stretchers.

1994

Kangchenjunga

The walkers danced. It was a ramblers' party.
The kilts and long skirts swung. The faces reddened.
He sat in shadow of an unlit corner,
looked at the floor but not the dancing feet.

The music stopped. Some jolly rambling ladies
accosted him, "D'you want a dancing partner?"
Slowly he shook his head and hardly smiled.
One said, "I hear you've just climbed Kangchenjunga?"
He barely nodded. In his eyes the blinding
cloud around Kangchenjunga. In his ears
winds screamed, and round about his heart there tightened
the ice of Kangchenjunga. Shifting legs
were shot with sharp reminders of his every step.

His wife, flushed from the dance, took friends aside
and said, "He wrecked his knees on Kangchenjunga
and now can hardly walk, let alone dance."

The band struck up again. The walkers' legs,
from Kent downs, or , at most, the Cumbrian fells,
moved in a rich design away from him.

Alone he'd won the peak, planted his boots
on the immense giant's head, his fairy tale
of solitary conquest, his supreme
creation, as though his own hands had carved
this glorious monument to climbing skill.

Fierce weathers, terrors or exhausted stumbling,
whether or not he'd reached the summit, none
were witnesses, except the Sherpas he'd employed.
He had not taken photographs: no proof
existed but in his sole memory,
for cameras always lied. No photograph
could reinvent the truth. It was enough
that he knew. Burdened by that knowledge, he withdrew.
Here in the afterworld, wakened by pain,
the bitter aftertaste of triumph silenced him.

Could he be thinking, in the rowdy room -
"Some reached their climax never to descend
to colour, shapes, laughter and questioning,
to comfortable house and patient wife,
to pain, wry proof of life, to sleepless nights
to Home Counties' snow, a week's prettiness
(with the mind's backdrop of exquisite blue-
green of a high crevasse, the whitening waves,
new snow caressing ancient ice and flowers
of new frost sprung upon the years of snow)

but stayed there, coffined in time-capsule ice...

"How can I take an old man's walking stick
and limp along the streets of Tunbridge Wells
instead of springing, leaping, whirling, high
as Kangchenjunga on remembered peaks?
How can I creep behind a shopping trolley
used as a zimmer? Should I stagger out
with my two Alpine snow poles, for a joke?"

1999

Some News Items
The Bouncy Church

Someone has invented
an inflatable church,
a take-anywhere
collapsible, portable
blow-up building,
complete with organ,
pews, pulpit, altar,
and a blow-up doll of a vicar.

Just think -
if you have one in your rucksack
when lost on a mountain,
or one in your car
when about to crash,
or a pocket-sized
mini version
when your team is about to lose,

you can whip it out,
blow it up. get inside,
say "Oh God" on your knees
and even be bounced up to heaven
where the bouncy angels are floating
like dolphin-shaped balloons.

2003

The Bread Summit

In the overfed USA
the former consumers
of bakery products
are dieting.
The bakers
of bread, the makers
of six-tier sandwiches
are worried.

They have organised a bread summit.

How about:
filling the bread vans
with all the stale,
unsold loaves,
unloading them in a desert
and piling them
up to the clouds?

This is a bread mountain.

One of the TV channels
could make a programme
of celebrities
in designer climbing gear

attempting to scale
the peak, competing to reach
the bread summit,

clawing their way up the crusts,
sinking to the knees
in the white sliced,
and then
scree-running down the granary,
abseiling on the rolls,
and finally landing
in the valley green with mildew.

2003

Winter Walking, USA

In Minneapolis in winter
they walk the malls
to escape the cold.
They drive to walk
between the shops,
several miles indoors.
Some walk one way,
some the other,
passing the same shops
again and again,
and crossing the routes
of the same walkers
at the same time
every day,
all these able-bodied
citizens, who never have to go
outside,
who never have to experience
air.

2005

Stogumber (for a guide to Somerset)

You get off the little steam train. There's a village deep in slumber.
It is Stogumber.

There is nowhere quite as silent from the Medway to the Humber
As still Stogumber.

Red houses in neat empty lanes suggest there is no lumber
Found in Stogumber.

A man stands on a ladder: he is one, the only number
Seen in Stogumber.

Though if they had a village dance they'd surely do the rumba
And wake Stogumber.

There's a "closed" sign on the only shop. The tearoom has gone
                                                            under,
Sunk in Stogumber.

But there's a genteel guest house that does sandwiches, cucumber,
Close by Stogumber.

In Somerset in August heat, the cottages burnt umber -
That was Stogumber.

Out There – Elsa Corbluth